Family Walks
in Gwent

Gordon Hindess

FAMILY WALKS

HIGH INTEREST · LOW MILEAGE

Scarthin Books of Cromford
Derbyshire
1995

Family Walks Series
General Editor: Norman Taylor

THE COUNTRY CODE

Guard against all risk of fire
Fasten all gates
Keep dogs under proper control
Keep to paths across farmland
Avoid damaging fences, hedges and walls
Leave no litter
Safeguard water supplies
Protect wildlife, plants and trees
Go carefully on country roads
Respect the life of the countryside

Published by Scarthin Books, Cromford, Derbyshire, 1995

Phototypesetting by Paragon Typesetters, Queensferry, Clwyd

Printed by Redwood Books

Photographs by Gordon Hindess

Illustrations by James Hindess (p36 & 60) and Michelle Hindess (p60)

Maps by Ivan Sendall

Cover photograph: Courtesy Islwyn Borough Council

ISBN 0 907758 87 8

Rhymney Valley Ridgeway (Route 6)

Preface

The sign that greets you on entering Wales across the Severn Bridge describes Gwent as the 'Gateway to South Wales'. But this hardly does the county justice: a gateway is for passing through, while this corner of the Principality offers much to linger and enjoy. There are mountains and hills etched by fast flowing rivers into deep valleys while, perversely, the River Usk meanders sedately across the middle of the county and the coastal levels provide a further contrast. The geology and soils are as varied as the topography, creating a delightful habitat for the natural historian to explore — can any county guarantee the range of birds that can be seen here? The hand of man, too, is evident — occasionally to excess, but generally adding a further dimension to the enjoyment of the rambler. The walks in this book will help you find the best of Gwent: the 'Gateway' is open, so come on in.

Acknowledgement

To the Art Department of the Bishop of Llandaff High School and, in particular, to Michelle Jarman and James Thomas whose sketches appear in the book.

About the Author

Gordon Hindess is married and his three children have grown up in South Wales, so this volume includes some of his own 'family walks'. Gordon is a chartered civil engineer for whom walking is the mental and physical therapy that counters the pressures of the working week. An interest in nature has been supplemented by an active study of the industrial archaeology and geology of South Wales. For some years, he has planned or led hikes for the local cubs, scouts, ventures and other groups and he is the author of the sister title 'Family Walks around Cardiff and the Valleys'.

Contents

Map of the area

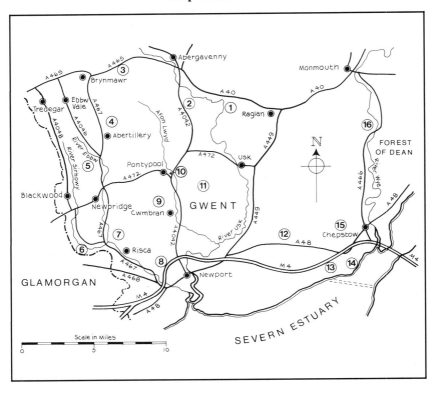

Introduction

The routes in this book have been chosen in that part of Gwent south of the A40. Unitary authorities threaten the disappearance of the County and its postal identification may well follow – but it will not be expunged from maps or the hearts of its population overnight.

Despite excluding the Black Mountains, the routes still rise to more than 1800 feet above sea level while, at the other extreme, the land is below the level of the highest tides. In between the scenery is surprisingly varied. In the north-west, the traditional industries of the coalfield have all but disappeared, nature is fighting back (with man's encouragement) and the inherent beauty of the area is shining through. To the south-west, Newport and its immediate hinterland is todays industrial focus, but with a bias towards 'clean high tech' employment on landscaped parks. The acclaimed Wye Valley marks the eastern boundary, but the majority of the area is occupied by the predominantly rural Vale of Usk, with its rolling hills, picturesque villages . . . and pleasant inns! The area has a rich history. The early residents erected their standing stones, while the Romans' legacy is more substantial and obvious at, for example, Caerleon and Caerwent and the Middle Ages have left their share of castles and churches. The heritage of the Industrial Revolution is not only of interest to the industrial archaeologist: reservoirs are now at the heart of country parks: the crumbling viaduct remains as a monument, blending gracefully into the landscape: and the disused railway, tramroad or canal is a linear nature reserve, a haven for plants and animals . . . and a walking route with the gentlest of gradients.

For children, a walk should be a mixture of fun and exploration – an adventure or an expedition. Involve them in route finding and seeking items of interest: for most routes, an unusual quest has been suggested. Encourage a child's curiosity and take time to answer questions, even if it means carrying a pocket guide to flowers, birds or whatever. Remember, too, that a family need not be restricted to two generations: granny and grandad often turn out to be walking encyclopaedias of natural history and may find a close affinity with their grandchildren in the countryside. The theme of a walk will depend on the interests of the party, the ages of children, the weather and the season, but the ingredients to suit all tastes and conditions abound in this book.

Choosing a Walk

If you walk regularly, you will have a good idea of your family's capability and should find it easy to select suitable routes from the Useful Information section which ranks them in order of difficulty. If you are not sure, then always go for a less strenuous option. The severity of a walk is subjective, taking account of length, amount of climbing (and its steepness and distribution) and the condition of paths. It is difficult to avoid hills in South Wales, so nearly all routes have some climbing. Do not be put off by this: just remember to take ascents at a comfortable speed with plenty of stops to enjoy the scenery. In most of the walks, a shorter variation is described so, if the going proves tougher than expected or the weather deteriorates, the trip can be curtailed without the frustration of retracing one's steps.

Timing

Allow time for the slowest member of the party not to feel rushed. With younger children, a mile an hour may be a realistic speed: by the time they are 10, 2 miles an hour may be achieved — but be sure to allow time for play, exploration and a lunch stop. Teenage children may need to accept that their parent's speed is the governing factor!

Clothing

Sensible footware is of prime importance. Regular walkers will undoubtedly go for proper boots but, in most cases, stout comfortable shoes will suffice and trainers may be preferred in dry conditions. Children may be happy in wellies, especially those for whom a muddy section would prove the highlight of the route. Comfort and a good grip are more important than expensive boots that will be too small in six months time. Remember that the weather can be deceptive and can change quickly — be prepared with jumpers and waterproofs, with the emphasis on layers of clothing to enable the optimum comfort level to be maintained, and take woolly hats and gloves in your rucksack, even if it seems warm enough at the start: there can be a world of difference between a sheltered valley and an exposed ridge.

Other Equipment

If you walk regularly, a rucksack is essential: it is by far the easiest way to carry things and leaves hands free for gates, stiles . . . and children! What goes in it? Waterproofs and spare clothing to start, then lunch if a picnic is planned. Even if not, it is a good idea to carry chocolate bars or other high calorie 'emergency' rations and a drink (hot in winter). Binoculars are very handy for identifying birds and distant features and a camera will record the highlights of a walk. While the sketch maps and route descriptions should prove more than adequate for navigation, many walkers will want to carry the local Ordnance Survey map (Landranger sheet references are given for each route) and, possibly, a compass. There are many good pocket guides on natural history to take as an aid to field identification. Finally, a small first aid kit is a good idea — children can be remarkably adept at falling over or getting stung.

Paths

In the main, routes use public footpaths, with a few permissive paths and waymarked trails in Forestry Commission or National Trust land, nature reserves and public parkland. Where roads are unavoidable, they are generally very quiet or have footpaths or good verges beside them. While signs and arrows may sometimes confirm the way, do not rely on these as the described route may be different and unmarked. Be wary, too, of recent changes — boundaries may come or go, stiles may replace gates, etc. Generally, the difference will be obvious with the way remaining self evident.

Refreshments

Nearly all of the walks have convenient pubs, teashops, etc on route. If they do not, suggestions for obtaining sustenance close by are made. Most pubs cater for children, although the only acceptable facilities may be outside tables. Muddy boots may not be welcome and it is polite to check with the proprietor before consuming your own food on his premises. There are official picnic sites on many of the routes or you may prefer to choose a convenient sheltered corner or viewpoint elsewhere . . . remembering, of course, to take your litter home with you.

Public Transport

Most of the walks are accessible by bus and, in two cases, by train. De-regulation has led to an increase in the number of bus companies with frequent changes to routes, timetables and operators. It is, therefore, advisable to check with companies in advance, particularly in the more remote locations. Public transport details, at the time of preparation of the walks, are given for each route, with bus company and British Rail particulars at the back of the book.

Clydach Gorge (Route 3)

Map Key

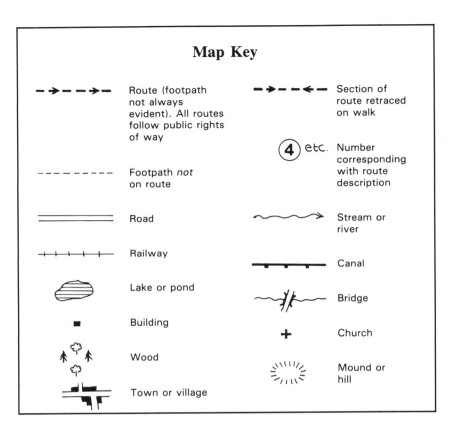

- ➤–➤–➤– Route (footpath not always evident). All routes follow public rights of way
- –––––– Footpath *not* on route
- ══════ Road
- ┼┼┼┼┼┼ Railway
- Lake or pond
- ▪ Building
- Wood
- Town or village

- ➤–➤–◄– Section of route retraced on walk
- (**4**) etc. Number corresponding with route description
- Stream or river
- Canal
- Bridge
- ✝ Church
- Mound or hill

Llandegfedd Reservoir (Route 11)

10

Clytha and Bettws Newydd

Outline

Clytha National Trust Car Park − Usk Valley Walk − Bettws Newydd − Coed y
Bwnydd − Clytha Castle − Car Park

Summary

The route follows the River Usk downstream for two miles, climbs gradually to
Bettws Newydd and Coed y Bwnydd hillfort, then returns via Clytha Castle. A varied
habitat attracts a wide range of birds and flowers and the landscape is a delight,
offering fine views on a clear day. The church in Bettws Newydd is particularly
interesting.

Attractions

This area was used as the setting for the television nature series 'Hundred Acres': it
is not hard to see why. Mallard breed along the river, which also attracts heron,
kingfisher, cormorant and sand martin. Various types of tit, wagtail, finch and
woodpecker can be seen and birds of prey are well represented by owls, kestrels,
buzzards and sparrowhawks. In the close season, a pheasant may be the bird most
easily spotted (and heard). Expect a wonderful display of flowers in the spring,
including primrose, lady's smock, stitchwort and wood sorrel, while the bluebells at
Coed y Bwnydd hillfort are spectacular. Later in the year, red campion, foxglove.
policeman's helmet, harebell and rosebay willow-herb may be found. Wild cherry,
with its distinctive white blossom, is prominent in April − but the birds will probably
beat you to the fruit! Look out, too, for mistletoe, high in the trees.

The un-dedicated church at Bettws Newydd (meaning new oratory) contains the
most complete rood loft and screen in Wales, dating from the 15th century and having
characteristically Welsh carving. However, children may be more intrigued by the
yew trees in the churchyard which, over the centuries, have sent up new trunks as
older parts have died back to create trees within trees. The 18th century folly, Clytha
Castle, is available for holiday-leasing from the Landmark Trust. The higher parts of
the walk look up the Usk Valley towards the Black Mountains: pick out Skirrid Fawr,
an outlier with a silhouette like a dormant dinosaur, the distinctive peak of The Sugar
Loaf and the rounded mass of Blorenge, marking the north-east corner of the South
Wales coalfield.

Refreshments

The Black Bear Inn at Bettws Newydd or the Chain Bridge (taking its name from the
adjacent structure over the river), ¼ mile down the road from point 2.

Route 1

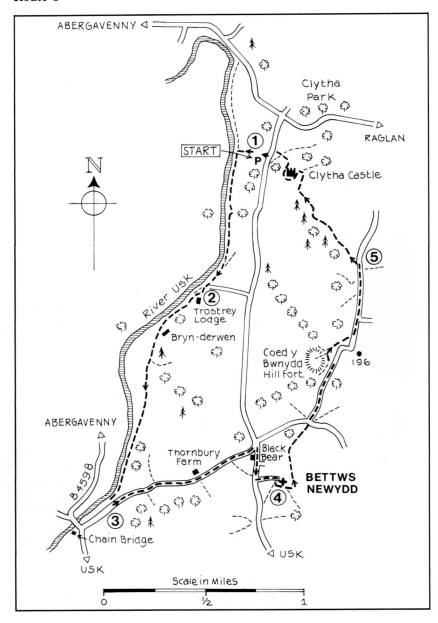

Route 1

Clytha and Bettws Newydd   5½ miles

Start

Clytha Picnic Site (National Trust): ¼ mile on right after leaving old Abergavenny – Raglan main road, opposite entrance to Clytha Park (OS Sheet 161 GR 361085).

Route

1. *Leave through a kissing gate at the north-west corner of the car park, follow a grass track to the river and cross a stile on the left (from here to point 3, the route follows the waymarked Wye Valley Walk). Follow the river bank, diverting only to use a gate at the end of the first long field. After crossing a stile, climb higher above the river, go over another stile then follow a field boundary to the right. Cross a stile to pass between a cottage and the steep drop to the river.*

2. *Go over a stile, right for 40 yards on a track then left on a grass drive. Pass to the right of a green barn and keep a fence on your right, crossing two stiles. Go over a stile on the right and head left diagonally down a field. Go through a kissing gate and continue on a path in front of Bryn-derwen. After the next kissing gate, bear right on a track, cross a stile by a gate and keep straight on. Continue through a gate with a fence on your right then along the bottom edge of a wooded bank, crossing two stiles. The path climbs through a larch wood then follows its top edge. Cross a stile and go left on a road. (The Chain Bridge is right.)*

3. *Follow the road for ¾ mile to Bettws Newydd. At a junction by The Black Bear Inn, go right then take the second road on the left (just after a golf club entrance on the right). At the end of the road, go into the churchyard.*

4. *Proceed around the church to the diagonally opposite corner of the churchyard, cross a stile and follow a wall round to the left. Go left up a track, cross a stile by a gate and continue up on the right of a field. Cross the next stile bearing right to keep a hedge on your right. Keep straight on over a stile and diagonally across a field. Go over a stile, left on a road and right at a junction. Follow the road up for ¼ mile, go through a gate on the left into the wooded area of the hillfort and bear right up to the top of the hill. Leave through a kissing gate on the right and cross a field, passing just to the left of a barn, to and over a stile on to a road. Go left, pass a road to the right and continue for ¼ mile until the road bends right.*

5. *Cross a stile on the left and follow a path to and over another stile: head left. Keeping a wood on your left and crossing a stile, go down two fields then follow the fence round to the right. Immediately past a gate, go left over a stile and keep to the left of a field. When the fence turns left, go right across the field. Cross a*

stile and follow a path through a wood. At a drive, go left and, just before Clytha Castle, take a path to the left, which then skirts the Castle. Go through a gate, left down some steps and continue to and through a gate on to a road. Go left, then right into the car park.

Access by Bus
Phil Anslow Travel Service 83 to entrance to Clytha Park.

Clythna Castle

Llanover

Outline
Ochram Brook — Monmouthshire & Brecon Canal — Llanover — Llanover Church — Ochram Brook

Summary
There are minor climbs near the beginning and end of the walk, but the majority of the route is sensibly flat. The canal offers splendid views as it wanders through meadow and woodland while, on the other side of Llanover, typical parkland scenery can be enjoyed. The shorter variation provides an opportunity to see more of the village.

Attractions
The main part of Llanover village centres on some older stone houses where the narrow valley of the Rhyd-y-Meirch (ford of the stallions) crosses the main road and a model village, Tre Elidyr. The latter is a unique memorial to the twenty villagers killed in the first world war: twenty houses built around a village green on which there is a war memorial in a semicircle of twenty lime trees. The remoteness of St Bartholomew's church indicates that the scattering of houses near the River Usk was once the core of the community.

Visitors to Llanover may be surprised by the absence of a pub in or near the village. This is due to Lady Llanover, a strict teatotaller and wife of the lord of the manor in the 19th century. In fact, one hostelry, the Goose and Cuckoo, does survive, high above the village, up a narrow dead-end lane, close to the western boundary of the parish.

The canal, opened in 1812, was the link between the Monmouthshire Canal, serving the industrial valleys, and the Brecon and Abergavenny Canal, which was initially used mainly for agricultural trade. For most of its route and here about 200 feet above the River Usk, the canal sticks rigidly to the same contour, avoiding any short cuts that might have required locks, aquaducts or tunnels. The absence of locks now appeals to leisure cruisers, while the crossing of the Ochram Brook is a good example of a meander resulting from hugging the contour. Along the canal, look out for slots for stop planks by bridges and a sluice for draining down the canal.

A wide range of trees and flowers can be found — see if you can spot thale cress, great mullein and ivy-leaved toadflax (in walls): in the early spring, daffodil and narcissus line some of the parkland drives. You may disturb a heron by the canal or along the streams, the chaffinch is common in the hedgerows, while wrens explore nooks and crannies in walls. Children will enjoy the newborn lambs in the spring and, if they fail to spot a rabbit on this walk, they should be made to go round again . . . quietly!

Continued on page 18

15

Route 2

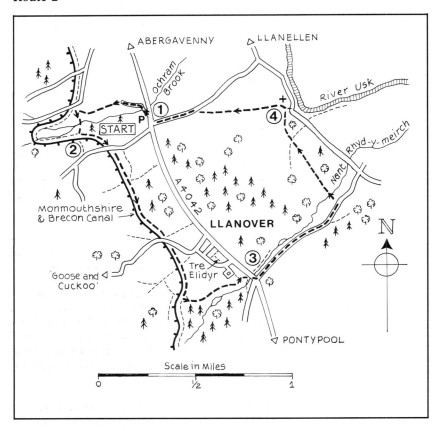

Route 2

Llanover

4½ miles
(shorter variation of 3½ miles)

Start

Stub of redundant main road, off A4042 just north of junctions, ½ mile north of Llanover (OS Sheet 161 GR 306093).

Route

1. *Go up the lane away from the main road and, at the farm, go left and through the first gate directly ahead to follow the top boundary of a field. Where the boundary turns right, bear right up to and over a stile in the far corner. Go left down an overgrown track, cross a stone slab footbridge and continue up to a bridge (No 85) over the canal. Join the towpath via a stile on the left of the bridge and head left.*

2. *Follow the towpath for a mile, passing under five bridges, then cross a stile on the left at the next bridge (No 79). Head away from the canal to meet and follow the edge of a wood on your right. Continue through two gates and down a grass track.*

3. *Pass a path on the left, go right on to a drive and left to the main road. Go right (note the picture over the Post Office door) and cross carefully to take a road to the left. Continue for ½ mile and, just past a gate house (Porth Gwenynyn), cross a stile on the left. Go straight ahead with a wall then a fence on your left, crossing a stone footbridge and three stiles. Continue over a drive, past a small garage, over a footbridge and through a gate. Bear slightly right across a field and go over a stile at the nearest corner of the churchyard.*

4. *Follow the path towards the church then take a path to the left and leave the churchyard via a stile in its north-west corner. Proceed, with a hedge on your right, through two gates and continue with a hedge on your left. Emerge, via a gate, on to a road and go left. At the main road, go right and cross carefully to the start.*

Variation

As for 1 and 2 above but, at 3, take a path to the left. Go straight through a small estate and left at a junction. Cross the grass on the right into the centre of Tre Elidyr and leave via a path on the left. Go right on a road, right at a junction and, at the main road, cross with care and head left out of the village. Just after a junction, cross the main road to complete.

Access by Bus

Red and White services 20 and 21 (with stops at the start and in the village allowing the option of a linear 2½ mile walk).

Refreshments

Explorers may try to find The Goose and Cuckoo. As an alternative, 2 miles to the south on the A4042 is The Goytre Arms — but why does its sign show a British soldier with a red indian squaw?

Monmouthshire & Brecon Canal

Footbridge over Ochram Brook

Clydach Gorge

Outline
Clydach Gorge Picnic Area — Clydach Ironworks — Cheltenham — Blackrock — Llanelli Hill — Twyn y Dinas — Clydach — Picnic Area

Summary
The route picks its way gradually up the gorge to Blackrock, but one strenuous climb up the south side of the gorge is inevitable. Thereafter, the going is easy. Cwm Clydach is a nature reserve, while the whole area is an industrial archaeologists delight: but it is the dramatic scenery which will make the greatest impression. The shorter variation halves the amount of climbing.

Attractions
The Clydach Gorge invited exploitation: it was the natural route for traffic from the Usk Valley into the industrial heart of South Wales and it had all the natural assets for local industrial development. The result was a steep-sided cleft crammed with railroads, tramroads, inclines, a turnpike road, an ironworks (employing over 1000 people at its peak), quarries, collieries, limeworks, a railway, cottages for the workforce, as well as pubs, chapels, etc. Today, apart from the 20th century's addition, the 'Heads of the Valleys' trunk road, all is quiet.

How could nature survive this onslaught? Remarkably well! Trees once again dominate the lower slopes, while scars have either healed or been adopted into an already rugged landscape to add to the drama of the scenery. While the route appears to comprise paths, tracks and little-used roads, it follows the tramroads, railroads, turnpike, inclines and railway for much of the way and passes the ironworks, two limeworks and a number of quarries. The walker should give free rein to his imagination . . . listen to the roar of the blast furnaces, . . . picture the pack mules pulling the 'trams', a steam locomotive labouring on the steep haul up to Brynmawr and the self-acting inclines, where falling full trams drew up empty ones on an endless chain: what mayhem might result if the chain broke?

But it does not require imagination to enjoy the birds, flowers and trees of the nature reserve that occupies the bottom of the gorge or the constantly changing and awesome views to be found around the route. Look down into the spectacular waterfall on the River Clydach as you cross Devil's Bridge at Blackrock, note the platforms that identify Clydach station and, for children, there are bananas to be seen growing in a rather unusual garden!

Refreshments
The Rock and Fountain Inn welcomes walkers and children (but booking for Sunday lunchtime is advised) and is well placed just before the main climb. Alternatively, there are barbecue facilities at the picnic site.

Route 3

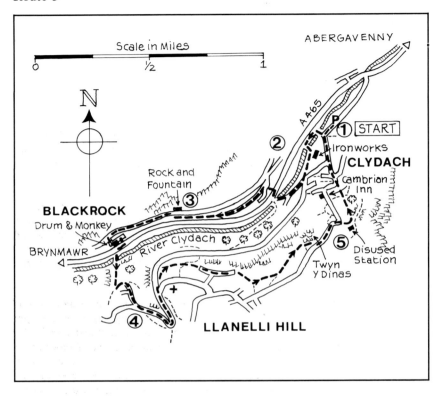

Route 3

Clydach Gorge

4 miles
(shorter variation of 1½ miles)

Start

Clydach Gorge Picnic Area: signed from A465, 1 mile west of Gilwern (OS Sheet 161 GR 231134).

Route

1. *Go right on leaving the car park and right at a junction. Cross the Clydach (Pant Glas Bridge) and take a track to the left. Go left, back over the river on the 1824 Smart's Bridge, pass to the right of the ironworks ruins and continue on a path (former incline) up to a road.*

2. *Take the lower road to the right. When it divides, keep right and, at the end, take a path to the right, through a gate. Cross the footbridge over the main road and continue up to a road. Go right then left at a junction. Pass a school and overgrown graveyard on your left and two paths rising on the right. Keep on as the road becomes a track then a path. Just after the second gate, take a path back up to the right. At the road, go left.*

3. *Follow the road, passing some limekilns, to Blackrock and take a narrow road down to the left. Just past the 'Drum and Monkey', go through a gate on the right, under the subway and right over a stile. The path drops down to and over Devil's Bridge (waterfall on left) then continues straight up the valley side (known as the Hundred Steps, though few are in evidence). After a short section between walls, cross a stile and go left on a track. Continue as it bends to the right and becomes a surfaced road. Keep straight ahead at a junction then go left at a T-junction.*

4. *Follow the road over the railway tunnels, round a hairpin bend and back on the other side of a valley. Pass a road to the right, then take a tarmac drive diverging right. Continue as it becomes a grass track, pass a path on the right then fork right, rising to a road via a gate. Go left, keep left at a junction and keep straight on when the road becomes a track. Take a path diverging left over a footbridge then heading back to the left through two gates. Keep straight on with a fence on your right then bear round to the left to continue with a wall on your right. Bear right then left around Twyn y Dinas, pass a path to the right and continue down to and over a stile on to a road. Go left. The road bends sharp right then, at a sharp left-hand bend, keep straight on along a track.*

5. *Pass between the station and old Railway Inn (dry!) and take a path on the left just before the viaduct. Drop steeply through woodland, pass a path to the right, cross a footbridge, pass a path to the left and continue down a narrow alley (beside*

'Troedyrhiw' with its unusual garden). At a road, go right then left at a T-junction and right at another junction. Keep straight on at the next junction and, at the bottom of the hill, turn right back to the car park.

Variation

As for 1 above but, at 2, take the higher road to the right. Pass Haulfryn then take a path to the left. At a road, go left and, at a T-junction, right by the 'Cambrian Inn'. Climb steeply, passing paths to left and right then, at a right-hand bend, take a track to the left and continue at 5.

Access by Bus

Service X4 (shared by three operators) stops on the A465 at the footbridge between points 2 and 3.

Clydach Ironworks

22

Cwmtillery

Outline

Cwmtillery Lakes Picnic Site — Mynydd Coety — Afon Tyleri and Reservoir — Picnic Site

Summary

After a fairly hard climb in the first mile to gain the heather moorland and views of Mynydd Coety, the going is easy. The shorter variation is much less demanding but, by starting at about 1000 feet above sea level, still tastes the atmosphere of a quiet mountain valley. The area has a rich natural history and clues to the valley's industrial past can be found.

Attractions

Once a busy mining valley, reclamation work has done much to restore its former rural character. But this is an area which is proud of its industrial heritage and the winding wheels of Cwmtillery Pit are preserved just south of the main lake. The route passes close by the entrance to an old level (now the source of a stream) at point 6 and another adit can be seen above the east side of the reservoir from the opposite side of the valley. Where the shales of old spoil heaps are exposed, you may be lucky to find a plant fossil.

The walk offers contrasting landscapes: the open moorland of the southern flank of Mynydd Coety: the narrow, wooded valley of the Afon Tyleri, north of the reservoir: the 300 feet sides of the natural amphitheatre of Pant Du (Black Hollow): the exposed cliffs above Cwmtillery West Side, marking the site of a landslip at the beginning of this century. The varied habitat is complimented by the flora and fauna. Enjoy the spring flowers in the valley, the moorland heather in summer and the trees in their autumn colours. Look out for a kestrel hovering on Mynydd Coety, or a buzzard gliding above the steeper valley sides, or just stop quietly for a few minutes in the valley bottom to appreciate the smaller woodland birds.

There are fine views of Cwm Tyleri and of the Afon Lwyd valley to the east. On clear days, the Brecon Beacons, Black Mountains and Mendips can be seen. A short diversion to the east just before reaching point 4 (the path is not very distinct) will allow a view over the ridge onto Blaenavon, with its famous 'Big Pit' just below the vantage point.

Refreshments

There are picnic tables by the car park or Abertillery has a good choice of eating places.

Route 4

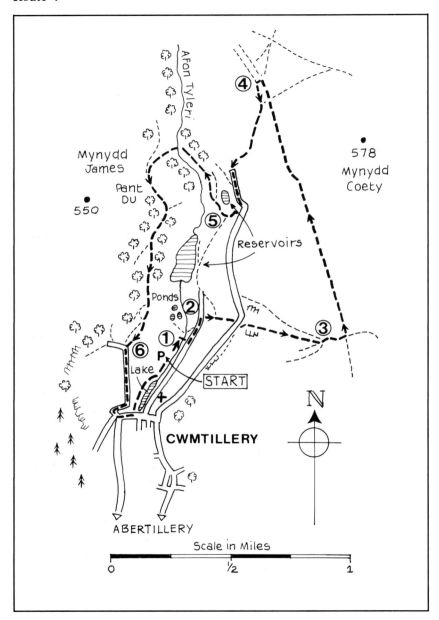

Route 4

Cwmtillery

6 miles
(shorter variation of 3 miles)

Start

Cwmtillery Lakes Picnic Site: from A467, follow signs to Cwmtillery then (brown signs) the Picnic Site — entrance is off reservoir access road above first lake (OS Sheet 161 GR 219065).

Route

1. *Return to the picnic site entrance and go left on the reservoir access road to a left hand bend.*

2. *Go right, over a stile and up a field. By a farm building, join a track and go left through a gate. Shortly, cross a stile on the right and ascend an avenue of beech trees. Go over a stile, up to a road and right 40 yards on this. Take a grass track sharply back on the left. The track quickly becomes a path, which soon rises steeply in the bottom of a narrow 'dry' valley. At the top of the valley, where the steep sides flatten out, go left on a crossing path to meet a prominent stoney track at a junction of tracks.*

3. *Go right on the stoney track and, at the crest of the ridge, head left on a crossing path. Keep to this path for nearly a mile, rising over a shoulder of Mynydd Coety then dropping down. At a low point, go left to join a track by the corner of a walled field and head left.*

4. *After ¼ mile, the track falls steeply then becomes surfaced and passes above an oval concrete reservoir. Just after a bend by a quarry, take a grass track sharply back on the right, down to and through a gate. Follow a path on the left of a stream (note iron oxide staining of bed) down to a track and go right.*

5. *Go over a stile by a gate and take a path diverging down to the left. Follow the most prominent path up the valley into and through a beech wood, to emerge via a stile into open land. The path crosses a footbridge and turns sharply left. Follow the path above some old spoil heaps and continue with a wall on your left. The path runs around the foot of Pant Du until it meets a grass track: go right. At a right-hand bend, take a path straight on. Rejoin the track, go left through a gate and keep to the main track as it meanders through an old quarry area. The track emerges into a field, turns left and then runs on the right of a ditch. When the ditch becomes concrete lined, bear right up to a tarmac track and go left.*

6. *Follow the track through one gate to a road. Keep left here and at the adjacent junction. Go through a kissing gate on the left and follow the path beside the lake and up to the car park.*

Variation

As for 1, but keep straight on. Pass Reservoir House and continue over a stile on the right of a gate. Follow a track through a gate and keep straight on, rising slightly. Cross a stile by a gate and continue on the track through another gate. When the track turns left on a bridge over a stream, continue as at 5 above.

Access by Bus

There are regular services (e.g. Henleys Bus Services Nos 1 and 7) through Cwmtillery, stopping by the lake.

Old Mine Adit

26

Pen-y-Fan Pond and Manmoel

Outline
Pen-y-Fan Pond − Mynydd Pen-y-Fan − Manmoel − Sirhowy Valley Walk − Pen-y-Fan Pond

Summary
An initial climb opens up views over the Ebbw Valley: thereafter the walk is easy going, apart from a short sharp rise out of the Sirhowy Valley. The pastoral landscape, with a wealth of trees, belies its elevation which is generally over 1000 feet and is home to a wide variety of birds. The shorter variation, on good tracks or quiet lanes, offers much of the flavour for less effort.

Attractions
Pen-y-Fan Pond was built at the beginning of the nineteenth century to supply the Crumlin Arm of the Monmouthshire Canal, although the water also drove the Ton-y-Felin mill on the way. Navigation on the canal ceased in 1930, but the Pond remains, providing a facility for sailing, canoeing, windsurfing and angling. The water also attracts birds (waders and competitors for the fish) while ponies can usually be found grazing in the surrounding park. You can also discover what an 'erratic' is here. The ¾ mile almost level circuit of the Pond may appeal to those with limited time or energy.

From the Pond to Manmoel, the ridge between the Ebbw and Sirhowy Valleys has escaped the excesses of industrialisation: it is possible here to imagine what the whole area would have been like had coal and iron not been exploited. Beech trees dominate the landscape, lining hedges, tracks and roads, and are a particular delight in the autumn. The quiet and observant may spot birds of all sizes from wren to buzzard while children may prefer to look out for the squirrels which abound. Manmoel nestles in the valley of a small tributary of the River Sirhowy: its children's play area may provide a welcome diversion for younger members of a family. From Manmoel, the route drops down into the Sirhowy Valley and a more varied habitat, with evidence of past mining activity.

During the walk, see if you can pick out two old churches, St Illtyd's, across the Ebbw Valley above Llanhilleth, and St Sannan's, at Bedwellty on the far side of the Sirhowy Valley. And is there a flying saucer not far from St Sannan's Church?

Refreshments
In the summer, a snack kiosk is open at Pen-y-Fan Pond. There are also picnic tables here and in the small playground opposite the Manmoel Inn which, unfortunately, is now dry.

Route 5

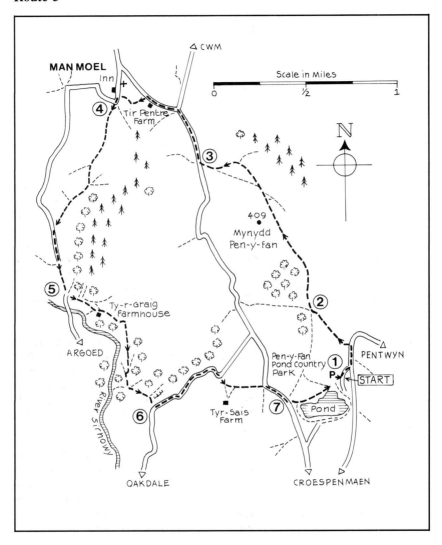

Route 5

Pen-y-Fan Pond and Manmoel

6 miles
(shorter variation of 2 miles)

Start

Pen-y-Fan Pond car park: turn north off the B4251 Crumlin-Oakdale road where signposted at Croespenmaen (OS Sheet 171 GR 197008).

Route

1. *From the car park entrance go left. At the T-junction, cross to the footpath, go left for 150 yards, then cross back to take a track to the left.*

2. *At a track junction go right. Keep straight on, passing through a gate then to the right of the summit of Mynydd Pen-y-Fan and through another gate. Keep to the main track, which falls steadily, turns left through a gate then bears right to a road.*

3. *Go right, pass a road to the right and, just after Tir Pentre farm, go through a kissing gate on the left. Keep straight ahead at the side of a field. At the corner, go right, over a stile, around the edge of a field and through a kissing gate to a road. Go left and, where the road bends sharply right, go straight on through a kissing gate. (The route now follows the waymarked Sirhowy Valley Walk to point 6.)*

4. *The path goes gradually up a field then follows its top boundary. Go through a kissing gate and continue in the same general direction. Keeping a field boundary on your left, continue through a gate then cross a stile on the left. Follow the field boundary down to another stile: cross this and go right on a grass track. Keep to this track, passing a track to the right and going through a gate, to reach a road. Go left. Where the road ends, keep straight on along a track which winds steeply down to the end of a road by a disused railway bridge.*

5. *Go left on a track which turns left and divides. Take the track through the gate on the right to Ty-r-Graig Farmhouse. Follow a path which skirts to the left of and just above the farm then continues along the side of the valley for ½ mile. Cross two stiles and, at a path junction, go left through an overgrown colliery site. At a track, go left and through a gate on the right of a stile. The track rises steeply, bends right by a disused quarry and emerges via a gate on to a road.*

6. *Follow the road to the left for ½ mile. At a sharp bend to the left, go straight ahead on the track to Tyr-Sais Farm. Take a track through a gate on the left and continue on it through two more gates at Tyr-Sais Stables. Go straight across two fields, passing through two gates, to reach a road on a bend (this section may be found diverted along the south and east boundaries of the fields). Go straight ahead.*

7. *Cross a stile on the left and bear right towards the Pond. Go left on the perimeter path back to the car park.*

Variation

As for 1 above but, at 2, go straight on through a gate and follow a track until it passes a house and emerges on to a road via a gate. Go left for ½ mile and complete the walk as at 7 above.

Access by Bus

Islwyn Borough Transport operates regular services through Croespenmaen, 1 mile from Pen-y-Fan Pond.

Near Mynydd Pen-y-fan

Sirhowy Valley Country Park

Outline
Pont Lawrence — Sirhowy Valley Walk — Ynysddu — Rhymney Valley Ridgeway
Walk — Mynydd y Grug — Ynys Hywel Farm — Pont Lawrence

Summary
The views from the Ridgeway Walk justify the stiff climb up from Ynysddu:
otherwise, the going is good and undemanding. A wonderfully varied habitat supports
a profuse array of birds, flowers and trees, while traditional breeds of sheep and cattle
are kept on Ynys Hywel farm. The shorter variation has only half the climbing of the
full route and it is better distributed.

Attractions
Today, it is hard to imagine this stretch of the Sirhowy as a heavily industrialised
valley: the railway has closed, but its trackbed remains to the advantage of walkers
and cyclists: the sterile river of a few years ago is now frequented by heron and
dipper. It is only on gaining the ridge between the Sirhowy and Rhymney Valleys that
a few spoil heaps give the game away: indeed, the summit of Mynydd y Grug is man
made! The Ynys Hywel Countryside Centre has adopted the redstart as a symbol. This
summer visitor is especially attracted to the area of ancient woodland south of the
centre and the male in breeding plummage has more striking colours than the more
familiar robin. Other summer visitors are flycatchers and warblers — the latter, unlike
good children, may be more readily heard than seen!

The Park boasts a particularly fine display of bluebells in May, colouring large
areas of the valley side. Among the many other flowers to be found, see if you can
spot comfrey. In the summer, you may be tempted by wild strawberries or
raspberries. This would be a good time to stimulate a child's interest in trees by seeing
how many can be identified, setting a target of at least twenty. There are more than
five species of conifer and the deciduous trees include some magnificent stands of
beech and the attractive rowan: as an added incentive, a bonus could be offered for
finding a bird cherry.

Between Cwmfelinfach and the starting point, Babell Chapel is passed. Its small
graveyard contains a monument to the 19th century preacher and poet, William
Thomas, known by his bardic title Islwyn.

Refreshments
The Ynysddu Hotel is well placed (requiring a minor detour) to provide sustenance
for the main climb. In the summer, the Countryside Centre offers tea with traditional
Welshcakes and there are barbecue facilities by the road on the last leg of the route.

Route 6

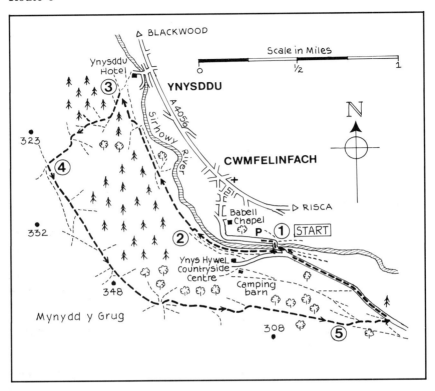

Route 6

Sirhowy Valley Country Park

5 miles
(shorter variation of 2 miles)

Start

Pont Lawrence linear car park: leave A4056 at Cwmfelinfach where signed to Babell Chapel and Ynys Hywel Countryside Centre (OS Sheet 171 GR 189912).

Route

1. *Cross the river bridge and, immediately, take the path to the right which is closest to the river. The path meanders across a steep slope, crossing several small streams before emerging on to a track, via a stile.*

2. *Go right. (From here to point 3 the route follows the waymarked Sirhowy Valley Walk.) After ¾ mile, just after a cottage on the right, take a path to the left. (For the Ynysddu Hotel, keep to the track here and, at a bridge, go down a path on the right.) After a few yards, go right at a path junction. At a path crossing, go left. (The path rising from the right comes from the bridge near the Ynysddu Hotel.)*

3. *At a path junction, keep straight on over a stream then take a path to the right, looking like a small dry stream channel. Pass paths to right and left then, at a path crossing, head left over a boardwalk. Go left at a path junction, fork right and head straight up the hillside. Cross a stile which forms an offset in a fenceline and continue straight uphill, with a broken line of trees on your right and crossing two stiles to reach a track. Go left.*

4. *(The route follows the waymarked Rhymney Valley Ridgeway Footpath from here to point 5.) Follow the track for a mile, adjacent to the top boundary of a forest and over a high point. At a multiple junction, take the left-most track and follow this round, just to the north of the ridge. Continue to and over a cattle grid. 300 yards after passing through the edge of a mature beech wood, take a path diverging down on the left.*

5. *Keep on to the bottom of the slope, then go left to and over a stile on to a road: head left. Keep straight on where a track crosses (barbecue site on left). Where the road converges with the disused railway track, cross on to it, go left a short way then down some steps on the right and keep straight on to rejoin the road. Go right, over a cattle grid and the river bridge to the car park.*

Variation

As for 1 above but, at 2, go straight across up a zig-zag path. (The route follows the Sirhowy Valley Walk to point 5.) At a junction, go left and, at the edge of the conifer forest, cross a stile. Keep straight on through a tree nursery and orchard and, at a road, go right. Take to the verge on the left and follow the fence. At a stepped path, go left up the hillside. At a path crossing, go left in front of a camping barn, continue to a track and head left. Take a path diverging right, then keep right at a junction to continue up with a fence on your left. Pass a path back to the right, cross a stile and go down to the left. Continue as at 5.

Access by Bus

Services 56 (Red and White) and 156 (Glyn Williams Travel) operate frequently through Cwmfelinfach.

Lower Sirhowy Valley

34

Cwmcarn

Outline

Cwmcarn Visitor Centre − Pontywaun − Southern Aspect of Medart − Pegwn-y-Bwlch − Twmbarlwm − Pegwn-y-Bwlch − Visitor Centre

Summary

This is a circumnavigation of the viewpoint hill of Medart, with a strenuous climb to the adjacent summit of Twmbarlwm, capped by a hillfort and motte. With a habitat ranging from meadow, through mixed woodland to open moor, a variety of birds and flowers is guaranteed. An easier alternative, combines a Scenic Drive with the last part of the walk.

Attractions

The valley of the Nant Carn, once dominated by a colliery, has been transformed by reclamation and afforestation. The seven mile Forest Drive, the first of its kind in the country, shows off the beauty of the valley today and takes full advantage of the spectacular views afforded by Medart, which overlooks the confluence of the Rivers Ebbw and Sirhowy. Along the Forest Drive are picnic and barbecue sites and childrens' play areas which may provide an attractive reward at the end of a walk. With a willing driver, the less energetic can combine both.

The earthworks of an Iron Age hillfort sit like a crown on the summit of Twmbarlwm, while the Norman motte at its eastern end is the pimple visible from much of southern Gwent. The views from the top are ample recompense for the stiff climb while, in the summer, bilberries in abundance offer a source of refreshment. The larch, spruce and Scots pine of the main forest are managed in a way that encourages wildlife. In the bottom of the valley and around the lower slopes of Medart, deciduous trees dominate while pasture and open moor add variety to the habitat encountered. On a fine spring day an almost continuous accompaniment of birdsong can be expected, the high-flying skylark taking his turn above Twmbarlwm. In the woodland, watch for the flash of bright yellow that characterises the rump of a green woodpecker beating a hasty retreat. On route to Pontywaun, terraced housing, typical of the coal mining valleys, can be seen − in particular, some with two storeys at the front and three at the back.

Refreshments

At the Visitor Centre coffee shop (weekends only) or nearby Tea Garden, where ducks are an added attraction. Alternatively, there are convenient pubs in Pontywaun and Crosskeys.

Route 7

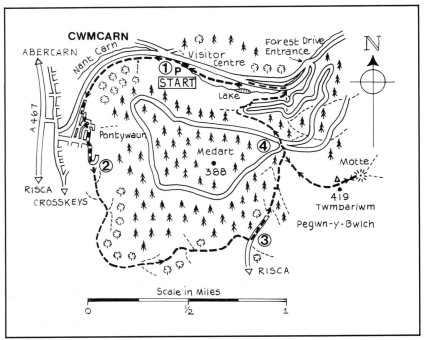

Woodpecker

Route 7

Cwmcarn

5 miles
(linear variation of 2 miles)

Start

Cwmcarn Visitor Centre: signed, with Forest Drive, from A467 a mile north of A4048 junction (OS Sheet 171 GR 230936).

Route

1. *Take a path down the valley on the left of the access road for ½ mile. Keep straight on when the path joins the end of a road at Pontywaun, then take the first left and follow the road round behind some houses. At a junction take the middle of three roads ahead, go almost straight ahead at the next junction (into Hillary Rise) and, at a T-junction, go left. When the road bends sharply back to the left, take a track straight ahead.*

2. *Pass a track to the left, cross a stile by a gate and continue on the track, passing a grass track on the right. At a sharp left-hand bend, take a grass track to the right with a fence on its right. Keep on past some old coal workings (marked by a spring), as the track becomes a path just above a coniferous wood. Pass a stile on the right then, immediately, fork right over a stile and keep straight on through a larch wood. At a path junction just after a stream crossing, go left. At a junction by a beech tree with a large hollow under it, head right, cross a stile and continue with a fence on your right. Drop down (still beside the fence) to cross a stile and a stream, then bear right on a rising path. Cross a stile on to a road and head left.*

3. *Just after the road becomes a track, take a lesser track diverging right. Keep straight on over a stile and, at a major track, go a few yards right then take a track back to the left. At a col (Pegwm-y-Bwlch), take a path to the right.*

4. *Climb to the summit of Twmbarlwm and continue past a triangulation pillar to the motte. Return on the same path to Pegwn-y-Bwlch and go over a stile on to the forest drive. Go right, cross the double junction carefully and take a path down steps on the left of a 'way out' sign. The path drops steeply to a track: go right. At the hairpin bend of a road, head left and shortly take a path diverging on the left. At a path crossing in a small valley, go left, over a stile and down a track to a road. Go left. Join a path alongside the lake and continue on it, between the stream and a caravan site, back to the Visitor Centre.*

Variation

Use the Forest Drive (for which there is a small charge per vehicle) to get to Pegwn-y-Bwlch, after the circuit of Medart, and leave the driver the chore of zig-zagging back down to the Visitor Centre. Cross the stile and follow the route from point 4.

Access by Bus

There are frequent bus services through Pontywaun (e.g. Glyn Williams Travel No.151) stopping near the entrance to the road to the Visitor Centre.

Cwmcarn Picnic Site

High Cross, Rogerstone

Outline
Fourteen Locks Canal Centre — Ynysyfro — Ridgeway — Sirhowy Valley Walk —
Canal Centre

Summary
After dropping down to the Ynysyfro Reservoirs, the walk crosses farmland before
climbing to the Ridgeway, with its splendid views. The return uses the Sirhowy Valley
Walk, crossing more fields then following the towpath by the locks climbing the
hillside back to the Canal Centre. The two variations reduce or eliminate the climbing
in the middle of the route.

Attractions
Water supply was always a problem for the Monmouthshire Canal and Thomas
Dadford designed an elaborate system of balancing ponds, culverts and weirs to
minimise wastage at Fourteen Locks. While none of the locks is functional and much
of the area is overgrown, exploration is still interesting and, possibly, even more of
an adventure for children. The locks enabled the canal to climb 168 feet in ½ mile
and the last barge passed through in 1930.

Despite its proximity to Newport, this walk has a rural atmosphere. The reservoirs
attract many birds — look for tufted duck, cormorant and pochard — while, for those
prepared to pause quietly, the hedgerows and woods are alive with smaller birds
including one of our smallest residents, the goldcrest. Children may find farm animals
of more interest; cows, sheep (with lambs in the spring), goats and chickens can be
seen, while many horses are kept in the area.

The Allt-yr-yn Nature Park occupies much of the area south of the canal at point
2 and the longer of the two variations meanders through this. But the whole walk can
be a showcase for spring flowers and a delight in autumn colours.

The Ridgeway offers views north over the Western Valleys of Gwent (pick out the
prominent hump of Twmbarlwm), eastwards up the Usk Valley and, to the south, over
Newport and the Bristol Channel. Can you spot the white clock tower of the Civic
Centre, St Woolo's Church and the famous Transporter Bridge. On a hot day,
youngsters who find out the name of No 5 deserve an ice cream at the end of the walk.

Refreshments
The Ridgeway park and the Canal Centre are fine for picnics — or the Rising Sun
is 400 yards westward along the towpath from the Centre.

Route 8

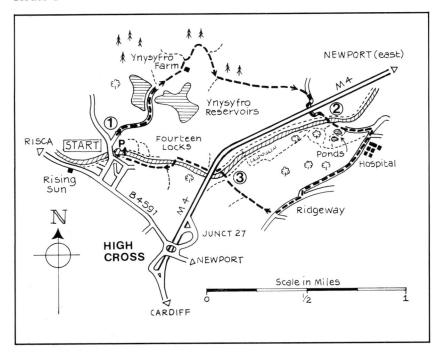

Route 8

High Cross, Rogerstone   **4 miles**
(shorter variations of 3½ and 3 miles)

Start

Fourteen Locks Canal Centre, High Cross: from M4 junction 27 take second right off B4591 (OS Sheet 171 GR 279886).

Route

1. *Leave the car park via the stile 40 yards north of the entrance. Follow the road right, down to and between the reservoirs. At the end of the dam, keep left and continue on the road to pass the cluster of houses at Ynysyfro Farm. The road becomes a track: follow this through a right-hand bend and, at a left-hand corner, bear right through a gate. Go straight across a field and through a gap in a hedge. Bear left to head down a field, keeping a wood about 50 yards to your left. Go through a gate and keep straight on to and through another gate. Bear right, go through a gate onto a farm drive and follow this to the right as it winds under the M4 and up to the Canal.*

2. *Go a few yards left on the towpath, then right over a bridge and follow a lane to the left. The lane rises to a T-junction. Go right, passing a road and hospital on your left, to the Ridgeway park. Keep to the grass just on the right of the roads. At the end of the parkland, go right down a track by a house and take the path (Sirhowy Valley Walk, which is now signed back to the Canal Centre) diverging left. Keep beside a wall, cross a stile and head down a field to pass to the left of a wooded gully. Go through a kissing gate and continue down to and through a similar gate. Cross a track, go over a canal bridge and head left.*

3. *Follow the towpath under the M4, past five locks, over the canal and beside eight more locks back to the Canal Centre.*

Variation

i   *As for 1 above then go left, right over a bridge and left down a lane. Just past a pond, cross a stile on the right and bear half right back to the pond. Go left alongside it then right between two ponds. At a path junction, go left, skirt around the second pond and go up to the right to reach a track, via a stile. Go right a short way, cross a stile on the left and head right up the side of a field. At the top, cross a stile on the right, go a few yards left and cross a stile on the left. Follow a path up the crest of a ridge and, as it levels out, take a path down to the right. Keep to this winding path with steps until it reaches a track. Go left a short distance, then right on a path which is bridged over the canal. Go left on the towpath and continue as 3 above.*

ii   *As for 1 above, then go right on the towpath for ½ mile and continue as at 3.*

Access by Bus

There are regular services from Newport on the B4591 (e.g. Glyn Williams X15) with the nearest stop ¼ mile from the Canal Centre.

Monmouthshire Canal

Fourteen Locks Canal Centre

Upper Cwmbran

Outline
Blaen Bran Picnic Site — Blaen Bran Reservoirs — Mynydd Twyn-glas — Mynydd Maen — The Square — Picnic Site

Summary
A long steady climb on the outward half of this circuit passes through attractive woodland and open moorland to gain some of the best views in southern Gwent. Nature lovers and children who enjoy an impromptu game of hide and seek should both find this walk to their liking. A less strenuous alternative route is suggested.

Attractions
A reclaimed coal spoil tip only five minutes drive from the centre of Cwmbran may not seem the most promising spot to start a walk. But do not be deterred, the industrial scars are soon left behind for more pleasant surroundings and the bustle of the town will seem miles away.

The Blaen Bran Reservoirs nestle in the head of a steep-sided valley in mixed woodland. The beech trees are particularly striking, with rows lining parts of the route or forming a canopy over it.

Ponies roam the moorland, while birds to look out for include the skylark and buzzard, the latter circling effortlessly on the updraft above the steeper valley sides. But the main reward for climbing on to the ridges linking Mynydd Maen and Mynydd Twyn-glas is the view: to the north are the hills between the Gwent Valleys: or look down into the deep, narrow and forest clad valleys of tributaries of the River Ebbw to the west: southwards, the hills of Somerset and Devon can be seen across the Severn Estuary: while to the east lie the valleys of the Afon Lwyd and River Usk with Llandegfedd Reservoir nestling in the hills between them.

The Square housed an early mining community, though only two of its sides remain today. Just before reaching The Square, as the route emerges from woodland into a field, look for the small craters of bell pits, simple shallow coal workings. Do not be surprised if children find the spoil heaps immediately around the car park an irrestible playground!

Refreshments
Families may prefer to combine this walk with a visit to the Greenmeadow Community Farm, a mile to the south, and eat there. However, The Queen and Bush Inn are close to the start.

Route 9

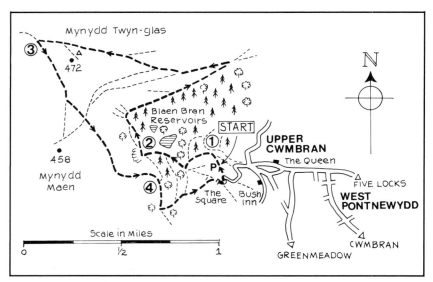

Boundary Post, Mynydd Twyn-glas

Route 9

Upper Cwmbran

4 miles
(shorter variation of 1½ miles)

Start

Blaen Bran Picnic Site: from Cwmbran town centre follow signs for West Pontnewydd, then Upper Cwmbran — the road narrows to single lane and entrance is track on right at sharp bend (OS Sheet 171 GR 271969).

Route

1. *From the north end of the parking area, go through a kissing gate and climb on a continuation of the entrance track. When the track divides, fork right, cross a stile by a gate and follow the track sharply round to the right. Cross a stile by a gate and keep on to a right-hand bend below a quarry face.*

2. *Continue on the track. Ignore all paths to the left as it again bends right and skirts the upper edge of a forest. Pass a path back to the left where the track levels out. At an oblique track crossing, head sharply back to the left. Climbing quite steeply now, keep generally straight ahead, passing two paths diverging to the left. Join a track and head left towards a radio mast. On your left, pass a triangulation point and a track.*

3. *By the radio mast, take a track to the left following a line of 'steel giants'. Immediately the track passes under the power lines, go left on a poorly defined path (evidenced by a shallow depression) back under the wires and continuing just on their left. At a track, go straight across on a clearer path. After turning left, the path drops steeply and, as it bends right, a path joins on the left.*

4. *Continue on what is now a track, cross a stile by a gate and a stream, then go over a stile on the left. Go straight down a field and, at a corner, cross a stile and the adjacent stream. Take a path forking right then, as the path swings left, take a less distinct path on the right down into a beech-filled ravine. Cross a stream, go left to and over a stile then keep straight ahead (area of bell pits). As you near the lower fence line, head for the right boundary, cross a stile and pass by a house into The Square. Take a track down to the left and, at the road, go left through a gate on a track back to the car park.*

Variation

As for 1 above, then take a path sharply back to the left. The path rises to meet a track; go left and continue at 4.

Access by Bus

Red and White service No.8 terminates 100 yards before the entrance to the Picnic Site.

Pontypool and Mamhilad

Outline

Pontymoel Canal Basin − Monmouthshire & Brecon Canal − Mamhilad − Roman Road − Ridgeway − Pontypool Park − Canal Basin

Summary

Following the level outward leg to Mamhilad there is a strenuous climb to the ridgeway: the rest is easy going. A number of interesting buildings and structures are passed, a wide range of plants and birds can be anticipated in the varied and mainly tranquil surroundings and there are good views from the ridgeway. A shorter variation is suggested.

Attractions

Pontymoel Basin is close to the southern limit of navigation on the canal today and marks the meeting point of the Monmouthshire and the Abergavenny and Brecon Canal Companies. Several original (and typical) canal bridges remain, but the aquaduct over the Afon Lwyd is perhaps the most impressive structure to be seen, though children may feel that this accolade should go to a tree-house in a garden by the canal. Roman engineers were responsible for the stone paving on the track which climbs up to the ridge west of Mamhilad. Despite centuries of neglect, particularly of the drainage, the main features of Roman road construction can still be seen. The folly watchtower at the high point of the route was taken down in 1940 so that it would not serve as a navigation aid to German bombers. Since then it has been marked by a simple memorial but, at the time of writing, a copy of the original tower is under construction.

Pontypool Park was laid out early in the 19th century by the wife of Capel Hanbury Leigh of the ironfounding family that was at the heart of the industrial development of the town. The same lady designed the grotto which is decorated inside with bones and shells. The route through the park passes under the dry ski slope, near the town rugby ground and a childrens' playground and leaves through the impressive iron gates, which date from the early 18th century.

The habitat on route is extremely varied and makes an ideal location for a field trip. Amongst the birds to look out for are heron, kingfisher, siskin and redpoll along the canal, tits and finches in the hedgerows, kestrel along the ridgeway, and woodpeckers in the park. Note the contrasting vegetation on the up- and down-slope sides of the canal: the alder, favouring saturated ground, predominates on the high side, while the well-drained towpath side has an almost endless variety of flowers and trees and is a good source of hazel nuts in the autumn. In this season, children may prefer looking for bigger nuts, from the horse and sweet chestnuts in the Park.

Refreshments

Horse and Jockey (leave the canal just before the bridge at point 2, go right down the road: return to the towpath on the path through the churchyard) or Star Inn at Mamhilad (keep on the towpath at point 3 to the next bridge and go right on the road: stick to the road on return to rejoin the route).

Monmouthshire & Brecon Canal

Sheep with lambs

47

Route 10

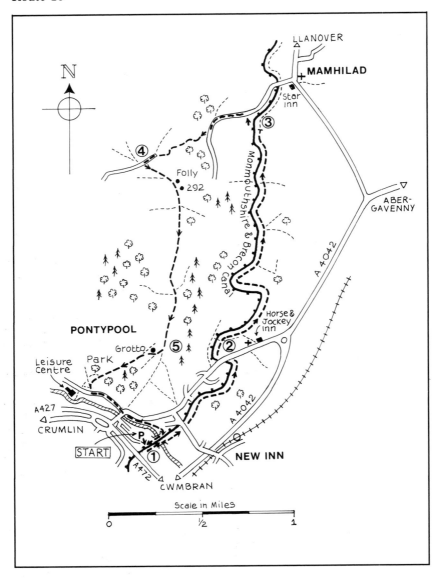

Route 10

Pontypool and Mamhilad

5½ miles
(shorter variation of 2½ miles)

Start

Pontymoel Canal Basin: take the New Inn road off the large roundabout on the A472 just south of Pontypool, turn first right twice (Fountain Road) and park on the right opposite Old Fire Station Garage (OS Sheet 171 GR 292002).

Route

1. Go over the canal bridge and left along the towpath, passing over the aquaduct, under a road bridge and through a cutting.

2. Go under the main road and continue on the towpath for a further 1½ miles, passing under five more bridges.

3. Go over the stile by bridge 61 (it has a deck of wooden planks) and cross the canal on it. Go through a gate and right across a field to emerge, via a gate, on a road: go left. Just after a left-hand bend, take a track (Roman road) to the right. The track climbs steeply to and through a gate into open land. Bear right up to a road, head left to the crest of the ridge and take a track to the left.

4. Go over a stone stile by a gate and continue along the ridgeway. The track passes to the right of the folly and swings right down to a gate. Cross the adjacent stile and keep to the track. Go over a stile by the next gate across the track and continue past tracks to the left and right. Pass to the left of 'Pen-y-parc', cross a stile by a gate and look for and go over an iron ladder stile on the right, into the Park.

5. Go over the crest of a ridge by the grotto and down a wide grass strip between conifer copses. At a track, go left and continue through a tunnel under the dry ski slope. Nearing the bottom of the hill, bear left down to a tarmac drive and go left on it. Go through the historic gates and straight across a road. Take a lane through garage premises which continues as a track with the Afon Lwyd on its right. At the end of the track, take a path to the right, up to the canal. Continue over the aquaduct and back to the Canal Basin.

Variation

As for 1 above but, at 2, leave the towpath and go left along the road, crossing when convenient. 60 yards before a mini-roundabout, go over a stile on the right and up a narrow strip of field between houses. Keep a hedge on your right, cross a stile then head obliquely up the hillside, crossing one stile, to meet a track by a gate. Go right over the adjacent stile, cross an iron ladder stile on the left and continue as at 5.

Access by Bus or Train

Several bus services stop at the end of Fountain Road (e.g. Red and White No 20). From Pontypool railway station (at New Inn), go right and right again at a main road: join the towpath where the road goes over the canal.

Ladder Stile, Pontypool Park

Llandegfedd

Outline

Llandegfedd Reservoir − Pentre-waun − The Forest − Llandegveth − Sor Brook − Reservoir

Summary

The route, mainly across meadowland, takes in a number of well distributed, and generally short, climbs. The one exception is the fairly stiff, ½ mile, ascent to the high point above The Forest: to avoid this, follow the longer of the two suggested variations. Bird lovers should find the walk particularly rewarding.

Attractions

Unusually for Wales, Llandegfedd Reservoir is at relatively low level (about 300 feet above sea level) and does not have a meaningful upland catchment: it depends on water pumped from the River Usk. Built to supply water to Cwmbran, Pontypool, Risca and parts of Newport and Cardiff, it is also a watersports centre with facilities for sailing, canoeing, windsurfing and sub-aqua. Fly-fishermen compete with heron, gull and cormorant for the trout, while various species of duck and over-wintering Bewick Swans can be seen. Elsewhere, a wide range of birds can be expected, but look out particularly for lapwing on the meadows or, perhaps, giving an exhibition of stunt flying.

If children do not see any rabbits, they should at least find their burrows: there are also badger setts close to the path north of Sor Brook Picnic Site. Wild flowers abound, with foxgloves prominent in the summer, when wild raspberries may also be found.

The triangulation point on the hill above The Forest is the highest point in an area bounded by the Afon Lwyd, Berthin Brook and River Usk. The walk down the ridge south-west from here gives fine views over the rolling, wooded hills that characterise this part of the Vale of Usk. In contrast, the narrow, steep-sided valley of the Sor Brook offers an intimate seclusion in a beautiful landscape. In Llandegveth (note the alternative anglicised spelling!), Court Perrot, home of a 17th century rector, is seen across the valley as a striking white house. If the shortest variation is followed, can you spot a link with Queen Victoria in Coed-y-paen?

Refreshments

The Farmers Arms in Llandegveth is close to the halfway point, while the Carpenter's Arms is convenient for the second variation. Alternatively, picnic by Sor Brook or the Reservoir, where there is also a kiosk selling snacks.

Route 11

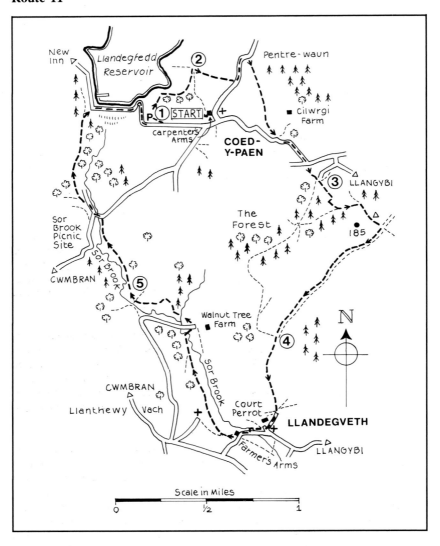

Route 11

Llandegfedd

7 miles
(shorter variations of 6½ and 1½ miles)

Start

Llandegfedd Reservoir East Side Picnic Site: signed from A4042, via New Inn, and second left after crossing dam (OS Sheet 171 GR 329886).

Route

1. *Walking parallel to the reservoir, go to the north end of the grassed area beyond the car park. Follow a path to the right at the bottom of a wooded slope, with a fence on your left. Go through a kissing gate, head for the far top corner of a field and, at an overgrown track, go right, through a gate.*

2. *Follow the track, through another gate, to a road and go left. At a left-hand bend, go right over a stile and bear left, obliquely up a slope. Pass to the left of a corner in a boundary and bear slightly right. Go through a gate to continue with a boundary on your left. Pass through a small gate and keep on by a broken hedge to the end of a field. Go left, through a hedge, and right, as close as practical to the edge of a field. Pass a disused quarry and cross a stile on to a drive. Go right, then left on a road. By a road junction, go over a stile on the right, cross a field and go over a stile (30 yards to right of a gate) on to a track.*

3. *Go left and through a gate on the right of a drive. The path rises on the left of a field, crosses a stile and continues in 'The Forest'. After right and left turns, join a track and go left. Pass a path to the right and, at a path crossing, go right to cross a stile by a gate. Keep straight on, at the edge of a field, over the crest of a hill. At the corner of the field, go right. The path keeps within fields, with a hedge on the left. Go over five stiles and through two gates to emerge on a track by a junction. Take the track almost straight ahead.*

4. *Continue downhill, through a gate and a farmyard and down a lane to a road. Go over the stile opposite, down the left side of a field and cross a stile and footbridge on the left. At a road, go right. Pass the Farmer's Arms and go right on a path by a row of firs to two stiles. Cross that on the right and follow a path down within a wood. Cross a stile and continue at the bottom of a field. Just before a wood, fork right. Cross a footbridge on the right then head left across a field. Go over a stile and head for the far right corner of a field. Continue over a stile and a footbridge: head right. Cross a stile by a gate, a road and the stile almost opposite. Bear left, keeping to the right of the valley floor. Go over a footbridge and a stile in the left-hand boundary. Go straight ahead, cross a stile on the right, climb through a narrow wood, cross a stile and go left beside a fence. Go through a gate,*

pass to the left of some barns, go through another gate, and bear left to join and follow a track. Go through a gate, and cross a track and stile.

5. The path keeps generally to the right of the valley floor, crossing a stile and a double stile. Continue up a long field then rise above the Brook to follow a track, through two gates, to a road. Go left then right into the Picnic Site, via a stile by a cattle grid. The path diverges slightly left from the access road, climbs the valley side ahead and continues across the top of a slope for ¼ mile. Cross a stile then, when the path divides, go right, down to the end of the dam. Cross the dam and follow the road to the car park.

Variation

i   As 1 and 2 but, at 3, go right. Where the track divides, keep straight on (almost level). After a mile, at a T-junction, go right and continue at 4.

ii As 1 but, at 2, go right again, through a gate and continue, keeping a fence on your right, through two more gates. The path goes left with a hedge on your left, crossing four stiles to reach the Carpenter's Arms. Go right on a road and right at a T-junction. After ¼ mile cross a stile on the right and go down a field to the car park.

Access by Bus
There are no bus services in the area.

Llandegveth Village

54

Wentwood and Penhow

Outline
Forresters' Oaks Picnic Site − Gray Hill − Llanvaches − Penhow − Whitebrook
− Picnic Site

Summary
Apart from a moderate climb around the flank of Mynydd Alltir-Fach, the uphill
sections are short and well dispersed. The route is mainly across farmland or along
quiet lanes, passing the tourist attraction of Penhow Castle, and other interesting
buildings and features, while fresh views are constantly unfolding. A short, but
strenuous, diversion to the summit of Gray Hill can be added.

Attractions
The entrance to the picnic site is thought to be the site of the medieval Forresters'
Oaks court, which administered the laws of the once extensive Wentwood Forest.
Wales' oldest lived-in castle, Penhow, dates from Norman times and was originally
the home of the Seymour family, perhaps best known for providing Henry VIII's third
wife, Jane. Do not be fooled into thinking that another castle has been drowned in
Wentwood Reservoir: the castellated stone structure is a functional draw-off tower.
Going back further in time, the stone circle and standing stones on Gray Hill are relics
of the Bronze Age. The stones may not be the most impressive examples of their kind,
but those with the time and energy to tackle this steep climb (adding a mile and 200
feet of climbing to the described route), will also be rewarded with superb views.
　　Limestone underlies the southern half of the route, causing dry valleys and streams
that appear only intermittently or unpredictably, depending on the weather. The route
passes through a varied habitat, which is reflected in the range of birds which may
be spotted. In the early summer, look for wild strawberries in road-side banks and
enjoy the scent of honeysuckle in the hedgerows.
　　Look out for the site of Llanvaches Castle (earthworks on the right just before
entering the village), the picturesque churches in Llanvaches and by Penhow Castle,
the former toll house on the 'old' main road, the remains of lime kilns (to the left,
¼ mile before Penhow village), the fish tanks and ponds at Whitebrook . . . and can
you find out who lives at 'Pike Den'?

Refreshments
The Rock and Fountain Inn is conveniently sited at the half way point (with a
welcoming log fire on chilly days).

Route 12

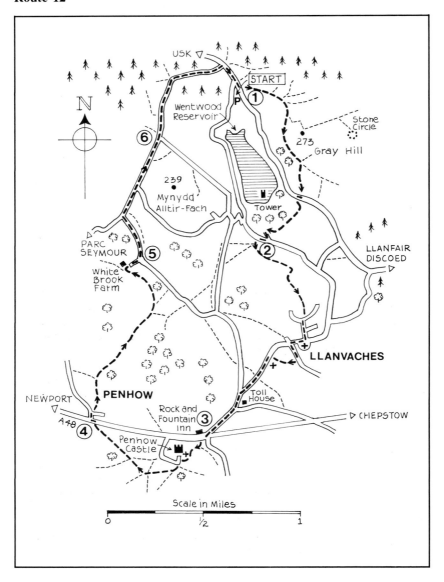

Route 12

Wentwood and Penhow

6½ miles
(shorter variation of 3 miles)

Start

Forresters' Oaks Picnic Site: follow signs for Llanfair Discoed then Wentwood from A48 east of Penhow and Site is just above reservoir (OS Sheet 171 GR 428939).

Route

1. *From the picnic site entrance go right and, immediately, left on a track. Continue through a gate and pass a track, path and drive on your left. Pass a path diverging to the left (this is the path to take for the 'optional extra' climb of Gray Hill) and, after ¼ mile (just after path coming down on left), go through a gate on the right. Descend the left side of a field to emerge, via a gate, on to a road. Go right a short distance, then cross a stile on the left. Cross a field and go through the gate on the right closest to the far corner. Follow the right-hand boundary, pass through two gates, then bear right, down to some railings. Go left over a stile, left on a drive and head right on a road.*

2. *After 150 yards, take a path back to the left, rising through a copse. Go over a stile into a field, bear left around a small group of trees and join a track with a hedge on its left. 40 yards from the end of the field, go right across it. Go over a stile into the corner of a field and bear left, bisecting the angle between boundaries. Over the brow of a hill head for and cross a stile in a corner. Bear slightly right to and over another stile to reach a road. Follow the road almost opposite to its end and go right. 50 yards past the church, take a road to the left. Near the last house on the left, go right through two gates. Keeping a boundary on your right, go over two stiles and down a drive to a road: go left. Pass a road to the right and, at a T-junction, head right.*

3. *From in front of the Inn, cross the main road, go down a bank and over a stile into a field, Cross a footbridge and bear right up to the left side of the church. Go over a stile, through the churchyard and a gate to the castle drive. Go left, then straight on through a gate on the left of a small barn. Follow the right-hand field boundary until it straightens then head down to a double field gate to the left of a drinking trough. Go through the gate then right, across a field, to the right corner of a copse. Go through a gate to follow a grassy track with a hedge on its right. Continue along the edge of a field and, via a short track and two gates, to the A48.*

4. *Cross the road, go left and, at a junction, right. At the next junction, go over a stile on the right and cross a field diagonally. Cross a footbridge, go left round the edge of a field and cross a stile by a gate. Head for and cross a footbridge and go right. Follow the valley bottom for ½ mile with a hedge or fence on your right, crossing two stiles adjacent to gates. On reaching White Brook Fish Farm, go through a gate and right, up the drive, to a road: go left.*

5. *At a T-junction, go right. Pass a road to the right and, at the next junction, go straight on.*

6. *Follow the road through the forest. At a T-junction, go right on a track in the right-hand verge. Cross a road to a path back to the picnic site.*

Variation

As for 1, then, just before a house on the right, take a road to the left, which zig-zags steeply uphill. At a T-junction, go right, pass a road to the left and continue for ½ mile. At a junction, go right and continue as at 6 above.

Access by Bus

Red and White and Shamrock Coaches service 73 operates on the A48, so start at Penhow village (point 4) or the Rock and Fountain Inn (point 3).

Forresters' Oaks Picnic Site

Caldicot and Caerwent

Outline
Caldicot Castle − Caerwent − Highmoor Hill − Caldicot − Caldicot Castle

Summary
From the Country Park at Caldicot Castle the route criss-crosses the Nedern Brook valley to Caerwent. The return includes a moderate climb to Highmoor Hill, a quiet lane along a low ridge and a surprisingly pleasant 'green corridor' through Caldicot. The route can be split into two half-length walks if desired.

Attractions
The 12th century Caldicot Castle was restored as a family home in the 19th century. It is now brought to life by displays and exhibitions or, if you really want to experience the medieval atmosphere, try one of the colourful, candlelit banquets in the Great Hall. The Castle stands in a Country Park: a pleasant spot for a picnic or quiet stroll, while children will enjoy the special play area or create their own games amongst the trees and embankments of the former moat.

The village of Caerwent sits on top of the Roman town of Venta Silurum and shares its main east-west street. Much of archaeological interest is hidden beneath houses and their gardens but, where excavations have taken place, an informal exhibition is only a peep over a fence or wall away! The Roman Temple can be seen 50 yards east of the church, while the remains of shops and houses are on the route out of Caerwent at the corner of Pound Lane. However, the town wall is the most striking legacy of Roman occupation: up to eight feet thick and as much as 15 feet high, it can be traced all round and much is open to public access.

The route passes through the graveyards of two 13th century churches, but the revolving lychgate in Caerwent may appeal most to younger members of a party. This is not just a walk back in time − the fields and hedgerows abound with birds and flowers: look for comfrey by the Nedern Brook and rock rose by the quarry. Glimpses of large buildings to the north may prompt a curious, but abortive, check on a map . . . for official cartographic purposes, Caerwent RAF base does not exist! Finally, the really observant should spot a tandem on route.

Refreshments
The Coach and Horses, Caerwent, and The Castle Inn, Caldicot: the latter, especially, welcomes children.

Route 13

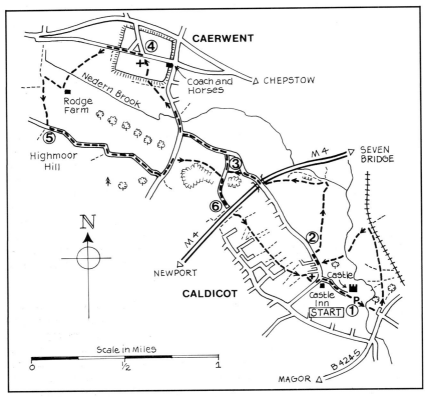

Caldicot Castle

Route 13

Caldicot and Caerwent   **6½ miles**
(shorter variations of 3 and 3½ miles)

Start

Caldicot Castle Country Park: signed from the A48 and B4245 (OS Sheet 171 GR 487884).

Route

1. *From the car park, follow the avenue (continuation of Country Park entrance drive) south-east. Go over the brook and out through the gate by a half-timbered lodge. Head left to cross a stile on the left at the end of a short cul de sac. Go right along the top of a steep wooded bank, to and over a stile. The path bends right, passing a path to the left, then left towards a gate. Before this, cross a stile on the right, go straight across a field and, crossing two stiles, through a band of trees. Bear slightly right across a field, go over a stile and straight on to meet, then follow, a fence. Cross a stile on the right and continue between two fences. Go over a stile and left on a track. Cross a stile by a gate, bear right and go over a footbridge. Keep straight on at the edge of a field, cross a stile and go right on a road for 100 yards. Go right through an opening in a wall.*

2. *Cross the farm storage area, go through a gate and head left (aim just right of barn). Cross a stile by a gate and bear right to and over a stile by a white post in the far boundary. Keep straight on to join and follow a field boundary. At the end of the field, cross a stile on the right and follow the hedge down and round to the left. Cross a stile on the left just before a footbridge, go left up a bank and then right. Keep straight on, with the top of a bank/hedge on your right and crossing three stiles, to reach a road. Go right, over the M4. Take a path on the right of the gate of the first house on the left. Follow the path between two fences to a road.*

3. *Go right and, at the T-junction, left. Pass a road to the left, cross the brook (dry in summer) and go left over a stile by the 'Caerwent' sign. Cross a field (aim just left of church), go over a stile then right on a track through the Roman wall. Cross a stile by a gate and go left over a stone stile. Go right, around the churchyard, through the lychgate and left on a road.*

4. *Leave the village and, just after West Gate Farm, cross a stile on the left. Head obliquely across three fields (aim for cluster of farm buildings across valley). After the third stile, cross a footbridge and go to and through a gate in a fence on the right. Head left through a gate on a farm track and, at a junction, go right. Just before a sharp right-hand bend, go left through a gate, up a field and through the left-most of a pair of gates. Continue between two fences, cross a stile by a gate*

and keep on uphill crossing a stile into a paddock. Keep on to and through a gate: go left on a road.

5. *At a T-junction, go left. After 150 yards, take a path to the right, by a quarry. At a road, head right.*

6. *Use the subway under the M4, take the second path left and head for a lone lamp-post. At a tarmac path, go right. Keep straight on along a 'green corridor', ignoring paths to either side. After passing a school playing-field, the path goes left and becomes a road. Go right through the churchyard, cross a road to the Country Park and follow the access drive to the car park.*

Variation
i *As for 1 and 2, then go left and continue as 6 above.*
ii *Park carefully in Sandy Lane near point 3 and proceed as 3, 4 and 5 above, but starting by heading north.*

Access by Bus or Train
Red and White services 59 and 64 stop by the town centre, ¼ mile from the Castle. The railway station is south of the town, a mile from the start.

Caldicot Castle

62

Portskewett and Mathern

Outline

Black Rock − St Pierre Pill − Mathern − St Pierre Park − Portskewett − Black Rock

Summary

Stroll the Severn shore and reflect on the ways used by successive generations to cross the Estuary. Mathern is reached across the Caldicot Levels while the return follows an undulating route through St Pierre Park. The walk explores the heritage of the area yet will appeal to the natural historian. Bird-watchers particularly may prefer the shorter variation.

Attractions

Black Rock was the ferry terminal for the South Wales railway until the Severn Tunnel was opened in 1886. The village of Sudbrook, ½ mile to the south-east along the coast, marks the end of the Tunnel and was built for the construction workers. Just beyond Sudbrook, the New Severn Crossing (due to be opened in 1996) can be seen while, up river, is the original Severn Bridge, opened in 1966. Each of these crossings represents an engineering triumph of its day.

Tewdric was a 6th century Celtic king mortally wounded in a battle with the Saxons. The spring in Mathern that bears his name is linked to his death and the 12th century church is his reputed burial place. The church is worthy of exploration and a brief guide can be found inside. Next to the church is the 14th century Bishop's Palace, while Moynes Court sits proudly on a nearby hill (though its tithe barn is in a sorry state). St Pierre claims the rather dubious privilege of having the only parish church in the middle of a golf course − but it was founded by a knight who crossed with William the Conqueror.

The Severn Estuary is a winter home for waders, such as dunlin and curlew. Heron, comorant and up to five species of gull may also be seen. Inland, the reens, hedgerows and woods are home to a wide variety of birds, including the brightly coloured goldfinch. Enjoy the flowers in the spring − not least, the glorious display of daffodils along the motorway where the route crosses over it − or the fine autumn colours in St Pierre Park.

Take care, especially with children, at the railway crossing by St Pierre Pill and on the short sections on the golf course.

Refreshments

The Miller's Arms in Mathern is a convenient half-way halt.

Route 14

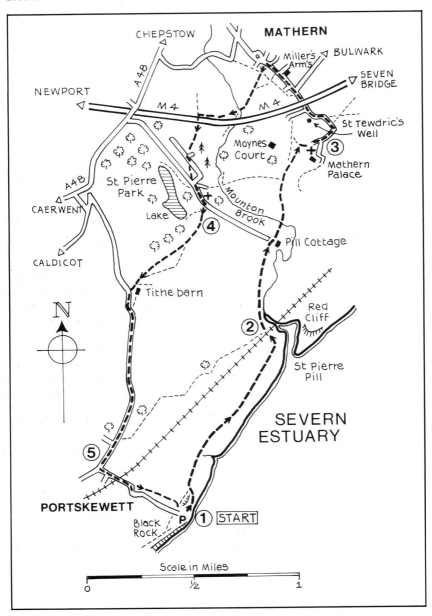

CHEPSTOW

MATHERN

Miller's Arm's ▽ BULWARK

A48

▽ SEVEN BRIDGE

NEWPORT ▽

M4   M4

St Tewdric's Well

Moynes Court

③

+ Mathern Palace

A48

St Pierre Park

CAERWENT ▽

Lake

+

Mounton Brook

④

Pill Cottage

CALDICOT ▽

Tithe barn

Red Cliff

N

②

St Pierre Pill

SEVERN ESTUARY

⑤

PORTSKEWETT

Black Rock

P ① START

Scale in Miles

0   ½   1

Route 14

Portskewett and Mathern

6 miles
(shorter variation of 2½ miles)

Start

Black Rock Picnic Site: signed 1st left at Portskewett, when approached from the A48 (OS Sheet 162 GR 513881).

Route

1. *From the disused slipway, head north-east on the coastal path. Cross in front of the red sandstone cliffs then bear left to meet a path on the top of the sea wall (an earth bank): go right. Cross a stile by a gate and continue until the sea wall turns inland at St Pierre Pill. Bear left to cross a white stile in the railway fence. Carefully cross the track and the stile beyond.*

2. *Go straight on at the edge of a field, cross a stile and continue across a field, bisecting the gap between reen and brook. Go over a stile by a gate then keep a fence on your left. Cross a footbridge and bear right towards Pill Cottage. Go over a stile, pass close to the front of the cottage and go through a gate. Keep a hedge on your left, go over a bridge over the brook then left over a footbridge. Turn right, skirt the golf course for 100 yards then cross a bridge and stile on the right. Cross a field diagonally and, at the far corner, go through a gate. Pass to the left of a small brick building, go right through a gate and follow a lane past the church.*

3. *Go left at a junction and follow the road, passing St Tewdric's Well on the left. Go under the M4 and keep straight on. Just after 'Bishop's Mead' on the right, go left up the drive of Glen View Cottage to and over a stile. Go straight down a field, through a gate, across another field and over a footbridge. Keep straight on to meet, then follow a fence and cross a stile. Go over a stile by a gate on the left, over the M4 and cross another stile. Go straight on (across golf practice area) to a drive junction at the right end of row of firs. Bear slightly left (crossing two fairways with care) to the car park at the end of an avenue of beech trees. Go left on a road, pass the church on your left and, just before the final golf complex building, take a track to the right.*

4. *At the first bend, bear off left on the left of a row of willows. Keep straight on through a band of trees, cross a stile and continue in a field with a fence on your left. Cross two more stiles to join a farm drive and follow this straight ahead. Go through a gate and, by a tithe barn, head right. At a road, go left for ¾ mile.*

5. *At Portskewett, turn into Black Rock Road. Pass a road to the right, go over a railway bridge then take a path diverging left at a right-hand bend. Go over a stile and continue beside the old track bed (barely discernible). Cross a stile at the left end of a fence and keep on a little to the left of a cutting. Go around the left end of a hedge and right over a stile by a gate. Go over a bridge, cross a stile by a gate and head left on a road back to the car park.*

Variation

As for 1 then, at 2, go left over a footbridge. Diverge slightly from the railway to cross a stile then head towards a small wood, passing through a gate and over a bridge and stile. Keep the wood then a field boundary on your right. At the end of the field, go through a gate then right at the edge of a field (the correct path is in a wooded strip on the right, but may be overgrown). Go through a gate and then left down a long narrow field. Cross a stile by a gate and go right on a track. At a road, go left and continue at 5.

Access by Bus

Red and White bus No. 59 stops at Black Rock Road junction. If starting here, the route can terminate at a bus stop 150 yards south of the tithe barn.

St. Pierre Church & House

66

Shirenewton and Mynydd-bach

Outline
Rhewl − Mounton Brook − Howick − Mynydd-bach − Shirenewton − Rhewl

Summary
This exploration of the valleys of the Mounton Brook and a 'dry' tributary and the twin villages of Mynydd-bach and Shirenewton, involves two climbs out of the Mounton Valley − the first long and gentle, the second short and sharp. The route is mainly in pleasant countryside with changing vistas and an abundance of wildlife. The shorter variation allows the villages to be by-passed.

Attractions
The church of St Thomas a' Becket in Shirenewton dates from the early 13th century: historians will link the date and dedication to the murder of the Archbishop of Canterbury in 1170. The solid tower is indicative of a Norman fortified church, though the arrow slits now support the spindles of the hands of the clock. While the only significant industry in the twin villages now is agriculture, there was a thriving paper making trade in the 18th and 19th centuries, with several mills along the Mounton Brook and evidence of these can be seen on the approach to Mynydd-bach. Many of the present buildings date from this period, not least the public houses . . . though some of these are now private houses.

Look out for for the imposing Itton Court on the hill west of Howick. The Grondra, too, has chosen the southern aspect of a hill and its walled garden displays the advantage of this: the passing walker, as well as the midday sun, get a good view!

The sparkling waters of the Mounton Brook give away their predominantly spring origin and the steep and wooded valley sides complete a quite idyllic setting for part of the walk. In the spring, carpets of celandine, wood anemone, bluebells and ramsons brighten up the woodland, while the trees themselves glow in the autumn. Ornithologists will enjoy the wide variety of birds which can be found, though children may prefer the farm animals (lambs guaranteed in the spring) and may just be lucky enough to spot a fox.

The higher points on the walk offer some delightful views − the Bristol Channel from Newport to the Severn Bridge, the limestone crags of the Wynd Cliff above the Wye Valley and the rolling Gwent hills.

Refreshments
There are three pubs on route (see map), but the Tan House will be preferred by families.

Route 15

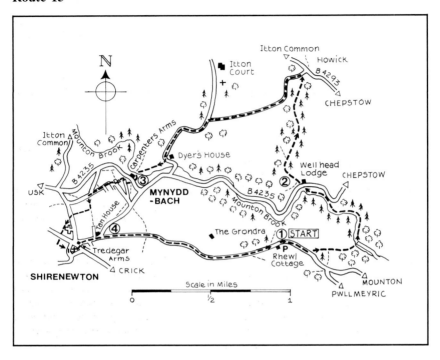

Route 15

Shirenewton and Mynydd-bach

6 miles
(shorter variation of 5 miles)

Start

Unusually large layby just east of Rhewl Cottage: 1½ miles on minor road off A48 opposite the New Inn, just west of Pwllmeyric (OS Sheets 162 & 171 GR 499936).

Route

1. *Go east on the road. Just after Rhewl Farm, cross a stile on the left to follow a path within the left edge of a wood. At a junction, keep straight on down a small valley to emerge from the wood near a cottage. Pass to the left of a fir hedge, cross the end of a road and a stile to follow a grass track. With the Brook on your left, cross two stiles beside gates, then head left. After passing through a gate, the path keeps generally on the right of the valley floor with the Brook to the left. Nearing Wellhead Lodge, go through a gate on the left, over a stile on the right and through a tunnel under a road.*

2. *Join a path and head right then, at a track, go left. After a right-hand bend, take a path to the right at a left-hand bend. After ½ mile in a wood, go over a stile and cross a field to reach a road via a gate by a house; go left. After ¾ mile, at a T-junction, head left. At the second sharp left-hand bend (below the white, 3-storey Dyer's House), take a track to the right. At a cottage, cross a stile by a gate and keep on along a grass track through a gate. Go left over a bridge, cross a stile and follow a track to the left up to a road.*

3. *Go right a few yards, cross the road carefully and go up a stepped path. At a road, go right and, at the end, take a path up to the left which becomes a drive. At a road, cross the village green diagonally to the gate of Rock House and take a path to the left. At a road, go straight on. Pass a road to the left and, just after a road back on the right, go left on a path. Cross a stile and keep to the right of a field. Just before the end, go right over a stile and follow a path skirting the lower boundary of a school. Leave the school grounds via a kissing gate and go over a stile to a road. Cross, go over a stile, bear left up a field to cross another stile and follow a path to a road. Go straight across on a path between houses and over two stiles to a road. Cross, go a few yards to the right and over a stile into a playing field. Cross to the far left corner, go up some steps and straight ahead on a drive to a road. Go right, then left into the churchyard. At a path junction, go left, down some steps and by the war memorial, to a road. Go down the road opposite, right at a junction and, at the junction just after Tan House, straight ahead.*

4. *Follow the road for 1¼ miles, passing The Grondra, to complete the route.*

Variation

As for 1 and 2 above but, at 3, cross to take a track to the left. At a road, go left to a junction then go left again. At a T-junction, cross to go over a stile. Go up a field, through a gate, and over the brow of a hill, to meet and follow a hedge on your left. Cross a stile, turn left and continue as at 4, but for a mile.

Access by Bus

Phil Anslow Travel service 63 stops by the Carpenters Arms (point 3) where the walk can be joined.

Mounton Brook

70

Trelleck

Outline
Pen-y-fan — Beacon Hill — Trelleck — Cleddon — Wye Valley Walk — Pen-y-fan

Summary
Undulating around the watershed between the rivers Wye and Usk with only gentle climbs, this walk offers distant views across the Vale of Usk and spectacular ones into the Wye Valley. There is much to explore in historic Trelleck, while the forest and farmland provide a varied flora and fauna.

Attractions
Trelleck takes its name from the three neolithic or bronze age standing stones, Harold's Stones, at the south of the village. But it is hard to believe that this small community was a borough in the middle ages and that magistrates sat here as recently as 1974. The church of St Nicholas, dating from the 14th century and with a 180 foot spire rising from an embattled tower, hints at a grander past: it has interesting stone and woodwork, an unusual sundial (inside the church, having been moved from its original site), and a preaching cross beside a massive stone altar. Terret Tump is the motte of a Norman fortification — could a modern house, let alone a wooden castle, fit on its flat top? The route out of the village passes the Virtous Well, a stone basin with seats where three or four springs with reputed healing properties emerge.

Early views are of the Forest of Dean, across the Wye Valley. Next the Vale of Usk appears, with the Black Mountains and hills of western Gwent forming the skyline. Finally, the Wye Valley Walk looks precipitously down on the tidal River Wye, some 750 feet below.

The forest sections will provide children with numerous opportunities for impromptu games and the fields are home to horses and other farm animals. The forest is more varied than most and the beeches on the steep sides of the Wye Valley, impressive at any time, can be spectacular in the autumn. Look out for the 2-3 feet high domes of pine-needles and other forest litter that are the nests of wood ants: it can be fascinating watching their activities for a while. Watch out, too, for the ghost of Lady Amberley who is reputed to ride the wooded slopes below Cleddon . . . though a more realistic quest for children is to find a Monkey Puzzle.

Refreshments
The Lion, at Trelleck: there is also the more 'up-market' Village Green Restaurant — though families may prefer an alfresco picnic by the Virtuous Well.

Route 16

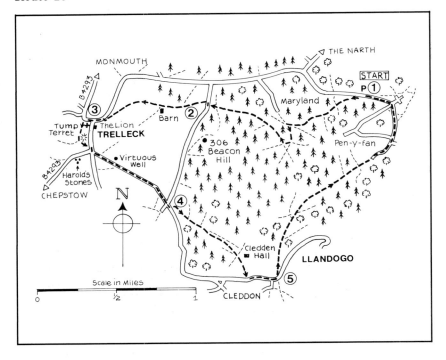

Route 16

Trelleck

6 miles
(shorter variation of 4½ miles)

Start

Manor Wood car park: leave B4293 at Trelleck (follow Pen-y-fan signs), take 3rd road to right and park is ½ mile on left (OS Sheet 162 GR 529059).

Route

1. *Go over a stile opposite and just west of the car park entrance. Follow a path into the forest, cross a stile and continue on a grass track to the right of a cottage. At a track junction, go straight across on a path. Pass a path to the left, go right at a junction then left on a track. At a junction, take a path to the right then go right at the first opportunity. Pass a path to the left, continue to a track junction and go straight ahead to a road.*

2. *Go right a few yards and cross a stile on the left. Cross a field, aiming for the distant steeple of Trelleck church (a general guide to Trelleck from here). Cross two stiles, pass to the right of some stables and continue down to and over a stile. Bear slightly right across a field, continue over a stile and, soon after a boundary joins from the left, go over a stile on the left: follow the hedge to the right. Go through a gate and bear left across a field. Go over a stile, down some steps and left on a road.*

3. *At a junction, go right and, at a sharp right-hand bend, cross carefully. Go through the right-hand gate to follow a track outside the churchyard wall. Go straight on over two stiles and circle to the opposite side of Tump Terret. Go over a stile, down a farm access road, left at a T-junction and right at a road. At a junction, go straight on then, immediately, left (Tintern Road). Pass the Virtuous Well and, ½ mile beyond, a road, both on the left.*

4. *50 yards on, take a track to the left which bends right and passes a cottage. Pass a path to the left at the corner of the forest. Go by a second path left, diverge right through a stone and earth wall and follow this to the left. The path bears right, is joined by a path from the right and meets a track, near Cleddon Hall. Go right, through a kissing gate on the left and head down to the lowest corner of a field. Go through a kissing gate and left on a road. Pass a road to the right and, immediately after a sharp bend left, take the track (Wye Valley Walk) diverging left.*

5. *Pass a path down to the right and, at a complex junction, take the second track right. Pass a path to the left, cross a stile by a gate, go through the next gate and continue on a road. Pass a narrow road to the right, go straight on at a junction and pass the Wye Valley Walk path diverging right. Go straight on at a cross roads and the car park is on the right.*

Variation

As for 1 above but, at 2, go left. Follow the road past Beacon Hill (the wooded summit does not offer better views) and down to a T-junction. Go left and continue as at 4.

Access by Bus

The route can be joined at Trelleck which is served by Red and White Coaches from Chepstow or Monmouth.

Virtuous Well

Preaching Cross & Altar

Toll House & Canal Bridge, Pontymoile (Route 10)

Useful information

Routes in order of difficulty

The following grading relates to a family with young children, not to seasoned adult walkers.

Easy:

Route 5 − Pen-y-Fan Pond and Manmoel (variation) − 2 miles
Route 14 − Portskewett and Mathern (variation) − 2½ miles
Route 13 − Caldicot and Caerwent (variation 1) − 3 miles
Route 13 − Caldicot and Caerwent (variation 2) − 3½ miles
Route 8 − High Cross, Rogerstone (variation 2) − 3 miles
Route 11 − Llandegfedd (variation 2) − 1½ miles
Route 3 − Clydach Gorge (variation) − 1½ miles
Route 9 − Upper Cwmbran (variation) − 1½ miles
Route 7 − Cwmcarn (linear variation) − 2 miles
Route 2 − Llanover (variation) − 3½ miles
Route 4 − Cwmtillery (variation) − 3 miles

Moderate:

Route 10 − Pontypool and Mamhilad (variation) − 2½ miles
Route 6 − Sirhowy Valley Country Park (variation) − 2 miles
Route 2 − Llanover − 4½ miles
Route 14 − Portskewett and Mathern − 6 miles
Route 16 − Trelleck (variation) − 4½ miles
Route 8 − High Cross, Rogerstone (variation 1) − 3½ miles
Route 12 − Wentwood and Penhow (variation) − 3 miles
Route 8 − High Cross, Rogerstone − 4 miles
Route 13 − Caldicot and Caerwent − 6½ miles
Route 15 − Shirenewton and Mynydd-bach (variation) − 5 miles
Route 16 − Trelleck − 6 miles
Route 9 − Upper Cwmbran − 4 miles
Route 1 − Clytha and Bettws Newydd − 5½ miles
Route 15 − Shirenewton and Mynydd-bach − 6 miles

More Strenuous:

Route 3 − Clydach Gorge − 4 miles
Route 10 − Pontypool and Mamhilad − 5½ miles
Route 6 − Sirhowy Valley Country Park − 5 miles
Route 5 − Pen-y-Fan Pond and Manmoel − 6 miles
Route 11 − Llandegfedd (variation 1) − 6½ miles
Route 4 − Cwmtillery − 6 miles
Route 12 − Wentwood and Penhow − 6½ miles
Route 7 − Cwmcarn − 5 miles
Route 11 − Llandegfedd − 7 miles

Public Transport

British Rail 01633 842222
Phil Anslow Travel 01495 792323
Glyn Williams Travel 01495 270489
Henleys Bus Services 01495 212288
Islwyn Borough Transport 01495 226622
Newport Transport 01633 262914
Red & White (East Gwent) 01633 485118
Red & White (West Gwent) 01495 270303
Shamrock Coaches 01633 251917

While the above provide services to the walks in this book, there are some 50 bus operators in the County. For further details, reference to the Gwent Public Transport Guide, produced by the County Council, is recommended.

Places of interest

Just in case it rains . . . the following are partly or completely under cover and should be of interest to the whole family.

Abergavenny Museum and Castle − presenting the story of this historic market town − 01873 854282
Beaufort Bird Gardens, Devauden, Chepstow − colourful attraction to delight all ages − 01291 5346
Big Pit, Blaenavon − unique underground museum in a real coal mine (children must be at least 5) − 01495 790311
Blaenafon Ironworks − best preserved 18/19th century ironworks − 01495 752036
Caldicot Castle and Country Park − Victorian house in a medieval castle − 01291 420241
Chepstow Castle − perched high on river cliffs to guard the river crossing − 01291 624065
Chepstow Museum − presenting the past of this once important port and market town − 01291 625981
Ffwrrwm, Caerleon − craft workshops, art gallery and restaurant − 01633 430777
Gelligroes Mill and Candle Workshops − wax artistry in an unexpectedly picturesque setting − 01495 222053
Greenmeadow Community Farm, Cwmbran − fun and excitement at a rural retreat in an urban setting − 01633 862202
Gwent Rural Life Museum, Usk − enchanting reminders of a rural past − 01291 673777
Legionary Museum, Caerleon − story of the Roman Garrison of Isca . . . with Amphitheatre and Barracks nearby − 01633 423134
Jigsaw World, Blaenavon − thousands of puzzle boxes and free browsing − 01495 791140
Model Farm Folk Museum, Wolvesnewton − Victorian nostalgia in superb country setting − 01291 5231
Nelson Museum & Local History Centre, Monmouth − find out why Monmouth has links with Henry V, Nelson and the Rolls Royce − 01600 713519
Newport Museum and Art Gallery, John Frost Square, Newport − the exciting growth of Newport from prehistoric times − 01633 840064
Penhow Castle − Wales' oldest lived-in castle − 01633 400800
Pontypool & Blaenavon Railway, Blaenavon − unlimited travel, but check steam days before visiting − 01495 792263
Raglan Castle − 15th century moated and fortified mansion − 01291 690228
Stuart Crystal, Chepstow − **hand produced fine crystal** − **01291 270135**
Tintern Abbey − impressive ruins in idyllic setting - 01291 689251
Tredegar House and Park, Newport − 17th century home of the Morgan dynasty − 01633 815880
Valley Inheritance, Pontypool − colourful story of a South Wales valley − 01495 752036

Workshop Gallery, Chepstow – watch distinctive pottery and intricate sculpture being crafted
– 01291 24836

Information offices
(Only Cwmcarn, Magor and Newport open all year)
    Abergavenny, The Bus Station – 01873 857588
    Chepstow, Castle Car Park – 01291 623772
    Cwmcarn, Visitor Centre – 01495 272001
    Monmouth, Shire Hall – 01600 713899
    Magor, M4 Services – 01633 881122
    Newport, Museum & Art Gallery – 01633 842962
    Tintern, Abbey – 01291 689431
    Tredegar, Bryn Bach Park – 01495 711816

Severn Shore, Black Rock (Route 14)

Some Welsh words of geographical significance

Aber — mouth (of river)
Afon — river
Bach (or fach) — small, little
Betws — oratory
Blaen — point, tip
Bryn — hill
Bwlch — gap, pass
Caer (or gaer) — fort
Capel — chapel
Castell — castle
Cefn — back, ridge
Coch — red
Coed — wood, trees
Croes (or groes) — cross
Cwm — valley
Cyhoeddus — public
Derwen (or deri) — oak tree
Dinas — city
Du — black
Eglwys — church
Ffynnon — well, spring
Glas — blue
Graig (or craig) — rock
Gwaelod — bottom
Heol — street, road
Isaf — lowest
Llan — enclosure, but commonly, church
Llwybr — footpath
Llwyn — grove, bush

Llyn — lake
Maen (or faen) — stone
Mawr (or fawr) — big, large
Melin (or felin) — mill
Moel (or foel) — bare hill
Mynydd — mountain
Nant — brook, stream
Neuadd — hall
Newydd — new
Pant — hollow, valley
Parc — park
Pen — top, head
Pont — bridge
Pwll — pit, pool
Rhaeadr (or Sgwd) — waterfall
Rhiw — hill
Rhyd — ford
Tarren — knoll, rock
Tir — land
Troed — foot
Twyn — hillock
Ty — house
Uchaf — highest
Y (or yr) — the
Ynys — island, meadow
Ysbyty — hospital
Ysgol — school
Ystrad — vale

Track on Mynydd Twyn-glas (Route 9)

THE FAMILY WALKS SERIES

The publishers welcome suggestions for future titles and will be pleased to consider manuscripts relating to Derbyshire from new and established authors.

Scarthin Books of Cromford, in the Peak District, are also leading new, second-hand and antiquarian booksellers, and are eager to purchase specialised material, both ancient and modern. Contact Dr. D.J. Mitchell 01629 823272.